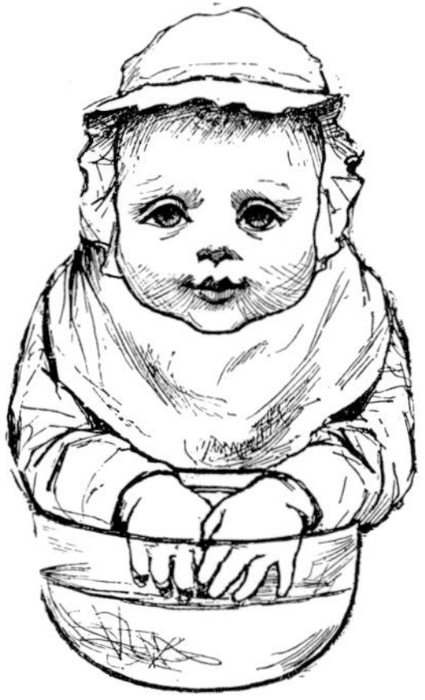

Keep me with you, for I bring
Good wishes, love and everything.

PEARS SOAP

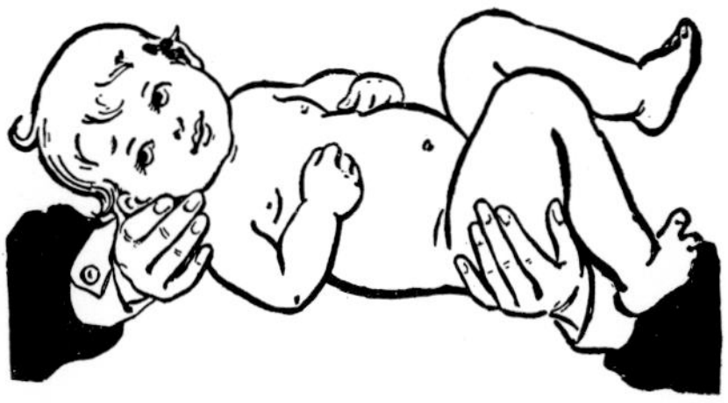

EDISON
TALKING DOLL

62

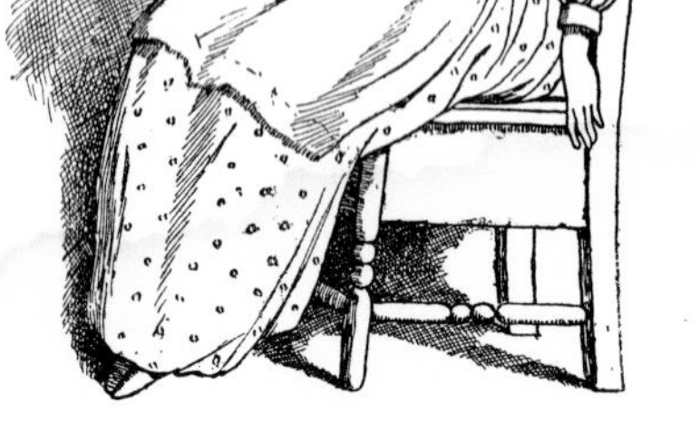
RAG DOLL

PUNCH & JUDY SHOW.

TINY TOWN

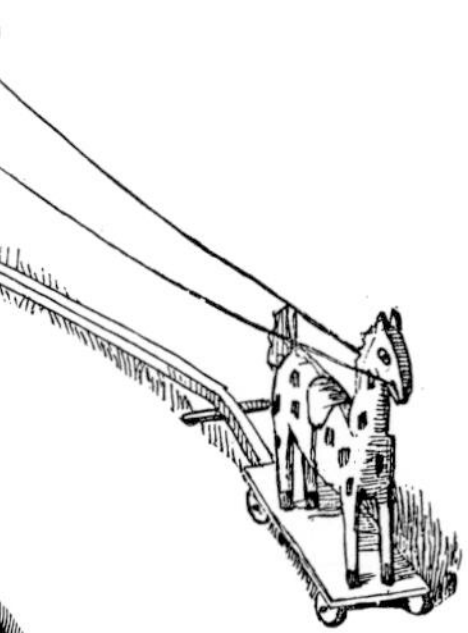

THE LATEST BOOKS
PERISHABLE
PERISHABLE

cat rat
do

LANGUAGE
LESSONS

LITTLE
WOMEN
LOUISA M ALCOTT

PECK'S BAD BOY
AND
HIS PA
COMPLETE

Elsie
Dinsmore
BY
MARTHA FINLEY

THE HOOSIER SCHOOL-BOY:
EDWARD EGGLESTON

ST NICHOLAS

HOOD'S
SARSAPARILLA
C.I. HOOD & CO.

TA-KA-KAKE
SUGAR CORN FLOUR

Tommy's
Circus

THE LOST LOVER
A FILM SENSATION

MEDICINE
CHEST.
SOOTHING SYRUP.
PEPPERMINT.
JAMAICA GINGER
PAREGORIC
OAT
MEAL

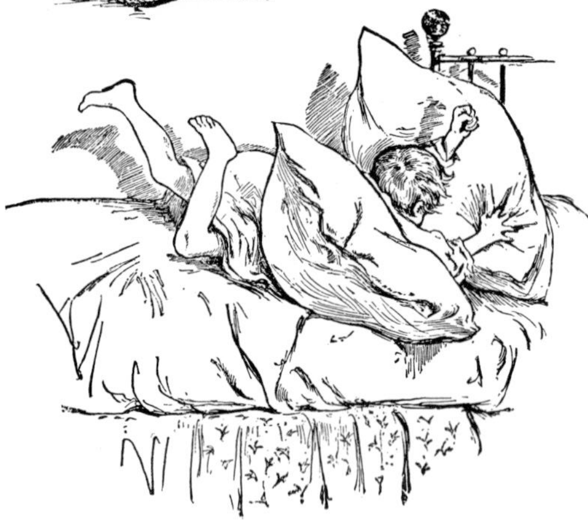

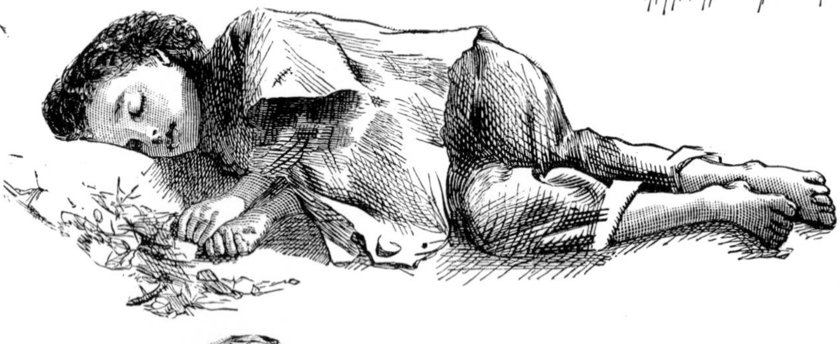

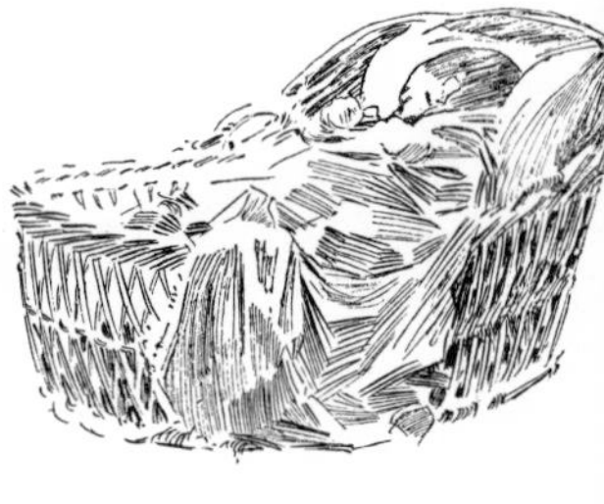

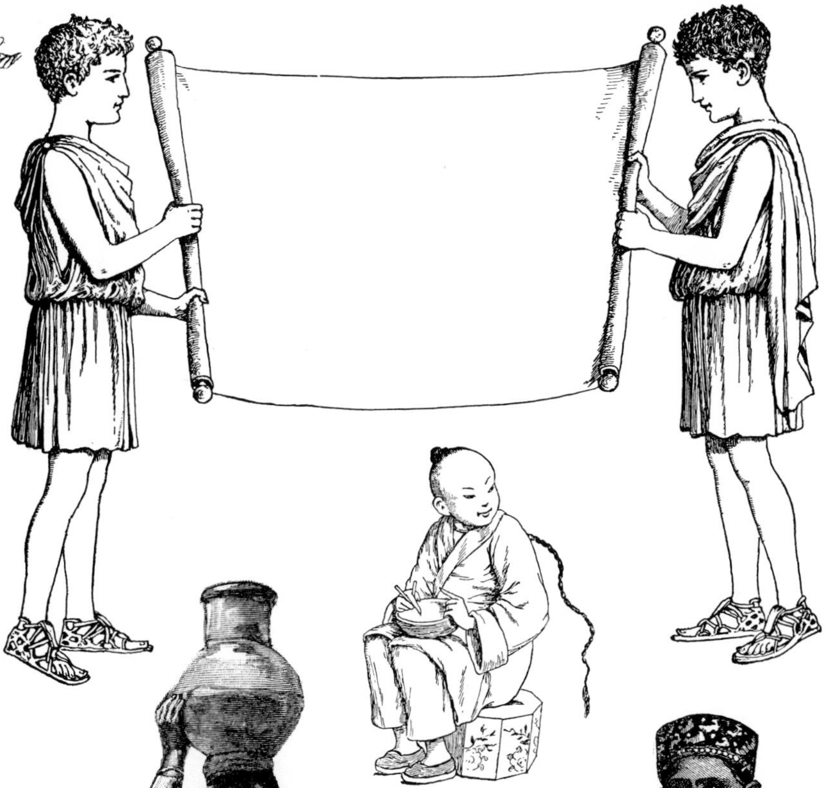